A RAGDOLL KITTEN CARE GUIDE

Bringing Your Ragdoll Kitten Home

By Jenny Dean

Table of Contents

Preface

A *Ragdoll Kitten Care Guide: Bringing Your Ragdoll Kitten Home* is the first in a series of eBooks that I will be releasing on Floppycats.com. For five years, I have not only studied, but I read, heard and experienced what it is to bring a Ragdoll kitten home.

If you read my website then you know that I brought my two Ragdoll cats, Charlie and Trigg, home from Soulmates Ragdolls in October and November of 2009, respectively.

Before that, however, I lived with my parents when they adopted two Ragdoll cats, Caymus and Murphy, from Bluegrass Rags in 2004. We also had Rags (the reason I was living at home at 25 – my mom wouldn't let me take him from the house) who was a 15 year old Ragdoll cat at the time.

Much of what I experienced taking care of all of these five Ragdoll cats is what I will talk about in this book.

Please enjoy this eBook and let me know if there are things you disagree with or if there are subjects you think I should make improvements to or expand upon – in fact, please email me with any questions at jenny@floppycats.com – I will do my best to respond with an answer.

I do ask that you please keep this eBook to yourself. I have spent years not only researching and gathering information but actually writing the book as well. My interest in selling this book is so that I can dedicate more of my time researching what the common person encounters with their Ragdoll cats.

The generosity of Ragdoll breeders with whom I have communicated via phone, in person or through e-mail over the past 10 years should not go unnoticed, their generosity of spirit, unending love for the breed and their attention to the breed have in part made this possible.

In particular, I want to give a huge thank you to Peg Nelson of Meriwidoz Ragdolls (retired), Jeanette Gogan-Olivier of Angelight Ragdolls, Andra Schroeder of Little Apple Ragdolls, Debbie Le-Strange of GUYSNDOLLS Ragdolls, Melissa Keefer of Pretty Kitty Ragdolls, who gave me additional information that I could add to this Book.

My vet, KC Cat Clinic (a feline specialty practice) has also been instrumental in helping me gain knowledge about overall cat health, well-being and care.

Please consider joining the Ragdoll Kitten Care Guide community on Facebook (http://on.fb.me/SQa1ch) or you can also join Floppycats on Facebook (http://on.fb.me/Oba0Ts), sign up for Floppycats newsletter (http://bit.ly/SCDUk7) or sign up to be a part of our forum (http://bit.ly/ObadG9).

Note: You are reading the hard copy of this book. This book was originally published as an eBook because with an eBook you have the capability to hyperlink to items on the Internet and it makes it easier to just click through and take a look. I reference quite a few websites, links to Floppycats and videos on Floppycats' YouTube channel throughout the book. If you contact me at jenny@floppycats.com I will send you a digital version of the book (in PDF form) that has all the clickable links - so that you don't have to spend your time searching and typing in links, rather you can just click through!

I have included "bitly" links and other shorten links throughout this hardcopy version of the book, so if you would like to type them into your Internet browser, they are available.

Introduction

Ragdoll kittens, like their adult counterparts, are usually very loving, placid and relaxed. They are quiet and playful. They are very intelligent and can easily be voice trained. Ragdoll cats are named as such because of their ability to go limp or flop like a child's Ragdoll (this isn't always guaranteed though – and I have received countless emails from readers of Floppy-cats.com who say their kitten is the exact opposite – so it's important to adopt from a recommended breeder (http://bit.ly/QYUnPa) or adopt an adult cat whose personality you can guarantee).

Ragdoll Kittens are usually born white (unless they are Mink in color). Ragdoll Kittens usually get their color and coat pattern as they age and their full color may not come in until two to three years of age.

Ragdolls come in several colors and patterns. The colors include (please note that you can see this same list on Floppycats.com – here's the link: http://bit.ly/PftfMT):

- Seal
- Blue
- Lilac
- Cream
- Flame or Red
- Chocolate
- Lynx (comes in each of the above colors and also in mink and solid)
- Mink (comes in each of the above colors)
- Solid or Non-Pointed (comes in each of the above colors except black takes the place of seal)
- Tortie (seal tortie or blue-cream tortie)
- Torbie (just like the seal or blue-cream torties except they have the lynx striping in their pattern) (The word "torbie" is a combination of two words - tortie and tabby)

Patterns include:

- Bicolor
- Color point
- Mitted

If a Ragdoll cat carries the white-spotting gene, then s/he may or may not have a blaze. Here are photos of Ragdoll cats with blazes (the kitten on the cover of this book, Charlie, has an hourglass blaze on his nose) - http://bit.ly/RjpdQ1.

You can see more photos and learn more about Ragdoll colors and patterns on Floppycats.com. Ragdolls don't reach full maturity until at least three years of age. Neutered males weigh about 15-20 pounds and are about three feet long. Spayed females weigh about 5 pounds less and are slightly shorter in length. Their fur is rabbit-like and medium long. All Ragdolls have beautiful blue eyes.

Kittens are released at approximately 10 to 16 weeks of age–depending on the breeder and the kitten (if s/he is ready to go). I am a firm believer that a kitten should not leave its mother before 12 weeks of age. There crucial developments that happen in kittens between 8-12 weeks of age. For example, they learn not to use their claws on their littermates and are therefore less likely to use them on you, furniture and the like!

Kittens are usually sold as one of the following:

- pet quality (a beautiful, loving kitten which may not be perfectly marked)
- show quality (closest to the Ragdoll show standard)
- breeding quality (a Ragdoll kitten that is suitable for breeding)

If you do not yet have a Ragdoll kitten, you can learn more about buying a Ragdoll cat on Floppycats.com.

Most breeders require a deposit for a kitten — usually when the kitten is still in its mom's belly. The deposit will hold your kitten of choice, until it is old enough to leave the cattery. Usually kittens are not reserved until a deposit is received.

Ragdolls should be purchased from a registered, reputable breeder. When a breeder decides to breed happy, healthy pedigreed Ragdolls, it's an expensive and timely undertaking. And that's why they charge the way they do!

Kittens should come with a sales contract with guarantees, and not "word of mouth" guarantees or health guarantees, etc. All guarantees should be in writing.

Occasionally breeders have older kitten(s) available due to someone changing their mind as to the sex and pattern they desired or simply because there haven't been buyers for that kitten.

Most breeders either have websites where you can see photos of the kitten or will email you photos of your kitten. Pictures of the kitten's parents are also sometimes helpful as an indicator of how the kitten will turn out – as far as size, type and style – however, the color and/or pattern of the mom and the dad might not be the color and/or pattern of your kitten.

Certain color and patterns when bred together produce certain color and patterns and you will want to know which color and pattern you like best.

Something else you want to take into consideration is what you are going to name your little one. There are ideas for Ragdoll cat names on Floppycats - http://bit.ly/Www5N5.

Getting a Ragdoll cat is at least a nine-15 year commitment (nine-15 years is the average lifespan of a purebred Ragdoll cat), but Ragdolls have been known to live a lot longer than 15 years. For example, my Rags died at 19 ½ years old! So this isn't a decision to be made lightly. You definitely want to be prepared and have thought out the next 15-20 years of your life as best as you can and see if your life and lifestyle will allow you to care for a cat.

Chapter 1

Kitten-Proofing and Preparing Your Home and "Safe" Room

Before your Ragdoll kitten comes home, you'll want to set up a room for your kitten – somewhere in your home where you will bring your kitten when you come home for the first time from the breeder. Make sure it is a peaceful, quiet place for your new baby. Anticipate your kitty being in this room for 1-2 weeks – this will depend not only on the kitty, but also if you have resident kitties, resident dogs or other pets as well as if you have children and how often you are home.

The reason for a separate room dedicated to your kitty is so that she or he can get used to the sounds and smells of your home as well as become comfortable enough that they want to play, eat, and go the bathroom and more. The less stressful the introduction, the better the chances are for long term happiness.

This room needs to have (don't worry I cover the specifics about these items later on):

- Food
- Water
- Litter Box with litter
- Toys
- Scratchers
- Grooming essentials
- Carrier

It's best if this room is a bedroom or somewhere quiet where your kitty can settle in and get used to his or her new surroundings.

You'll want to kitten-proof your home – think of it as baby-proofing your home. Kittens are curious and mischievous. You'll want to make sure you tie up or put away the following:

- Cords on blinds
- Electrical cords
- Poisonous plants – all lilies, amaryllis, English ivy, philodendrons, poinsettias
- Anti-freeze
- Cleaning supplies

- Rat killer/bait and other poisons
- Aspirin
- Tylenol
- Strings
- Needles
- Sewing Supplies
- Christmas decorations - such as icicles and breakable baubles (and hooks)
- Yarn
- Coins
- Rubber and hair bands
- Balloons
- Cotton Balls

You also want to make an appointment with your veterinarian. If this is your first cat and you don't have a vet, then you will want to get a recommendation for a vet. Ask a neighbor, a friend or a family member where they take their pets – be sure to ask someone that takes care of their animals like you take care or plan to take care of your cat. There are regular vets, specialty vets and holistic vets practicing in all areas.

Once you have found a vet – ask the vet questions about their business whether walk-ins are permitted and about emergency clinics and services. It's best to be prepared because you never know when an emergency may occur with your kitten. It might be best if you make an appointment to just talk with your new vet and let them know you will soon be getting a kitten. Have a list of concerns to ask the vet. That way, you will get a good feeling (or not) about any new potential vet and their staff.

My mom actually has one of those label makers and she used it to type out the emergency vet's name and number in case there is ever an emergency with any of her animals. She then put the label on every phone in the kitchen and then at strategic phones throughout her home. I know the number by heart but since there are so many people in and out of my parents' home – she wanted it everywhere.

You definitely also want to know the Animal Poison Control Center's number for your country. For the United States it is (888) 426-4435. They are the best resource for any animal poison-related emergency, 24 hours a day, 365 days a year. Be aware that as of March 2011, a $65 consultation fee may be applied to your credit card. Some microchip companies offer free, 24/7 ASPCA-certified veterinary consults with a subscription (i.e. Home Again).

After you've done your shopping and have chosen your vet – take a good look at your home from your kitten's perspective. Believe me, it will not be a bad idea to get down on the ground and look at things from a kitten's point of view.

Think of it as toddler-proofing. Look for small spaces that a kitten may hide or get stuck in. Move breakables to a safe place, check for loose cables and electric wires. If you have pull blinds on the windows, you might tie them up (I just made them high enough so that the kitties couldn't reach them) or you can get child-proof tubes to put around them at one of the home improvement stores.

If your kitten is a "wire or cord" chew-er you can protect your electric cords and computer cables - and your kitten- with the same plastic tube covers discussed above that are available at home improvement stores. Wall socket plug covers are cheap, easy to install, and will keep paws safe.

Keep string, yarn, thread or ribbons in a container or a drawer that your kitty cannot access when not in use.

Be sure to close all drawers and cabinets completely – kittens may jump into ajar drawers and get stuck behind them, or find dangerous items inside cabinets.

Be sure to check out the Bringing Your Ragdoll Kitten Home – Checklist at the end of the eBook. You can print it separately and bring it to the store with you.

Chapter 2

First Days with Your Kitten and Things to Watch Out For

First Days

The first few days may be difficult for your Ragdoll baby; after all, he/she has been used to his or her mom, brothers and sisters in a family environment. Suddenly they are not there anymore – so your new kitten might cry and call for them. Likewise, the sights, sounds and smells of your home might make for a few initial nervous days - it takes time to adjust to his/her new home and your patience and tender care are needed.

Other than missing their mom, brothers and sisters, when buying a Ragdoll kitten from a reputable breeder, more than likely you will not have many issues the first few days. In fact, Ragdoll kittens adapt to their new homes quite easily. However some of them might take just a little bit more time to adjust to their new surroundings and you need to be patient and loving during this phase.

The best time to bring a new ragdoll kitten into the household is when you will be off from work for a few days, like getting the kitten on a Friday so that you have all weekend to acclimate this precious new member of your family.

If you are getting your kitten shipped to you – your breeder will know about the particulars and more than likely you will pick up your kitten in the cargo area of your airport.

If you are picking up your kitten, then you will need to check with the airlines to see what their requirements are as far as carriers, flights and restrictions. Some airlines only allow so many carry-on pets per flight. You also will need to pay additional fees.

The time your kitten needs to adjust to your home will vary depending on the personality of the kitten. For example, when I brought Charlie home (October 15, 2009), he burst out of his carrier and ran around the room (my bedroom); he played with me and my boyfriend and then eventually decided to eat. This was just the beginning signs of his outgoing personality. And, of course, I had told my boyfriend that he would probably hide and be scared – NOT A CHANCE with Charlie.

When I brought Trigg home (November 8, 2009), he didn't want to get out of his carrier – and I shouldn't have forced him to get out, but I did and he quickly found refuge under the bed (his "safe" room was the guest bedroom and my boyfriend slept in there with him). **He took about 24 hours to go the bathroom and to eat. This is not terribly uncommon, depending on stress of the trip and maturity of the cat/kitten.** Once they eat and use their box, you know they are starting to settle in at their new home!

Charlie's reaction was totally different than what I expected. I expected Trigg's reaction from both of them because they had been in a carrier for 10 hours, flew on an airplane, walked around the airport and then finally came to a place that didn't smell or look like their previous home.

Trigg's reaction was more of the cat reaction I was accustomed to! So I guess you never know what to expect, so just be soft, gentle and sensitive with your new babe and allow them to teach you their personality.

When you get home with your kitten, go straight to their "safe" room (no other animals should be in this room) and place the carrier (with the kitten inside of it) in the room you prepared. **Open the door of the carrier and let your new kitten come out when s/he is ready.** You might consider taking the door off the carrier; so that the kitten can come and go from this carrier as s/he wishes (much like Trigg did with the bed) – sometimes doors of carriers will close with gravity – so that's why it's sometimes wiser to just take off the door altogether.

Spend time with your kitten in this room for the first few hours – ever heard the expression, "Curiosity killed the cat"? Well, your kitten comes with built-in curiosity, so s/he will come out of the carrier in due time, when s/he is comfortable enough to explore new surroundings. If possible, get down on the floor to talk to and to play with the kitten – you being down on their level provides added security.

Show your new kitten where the food and water bowls are as well as the litter box (don't put the litter box next to the food and water bowls – but rather at least 5 feet away – would you want to eat next to a toilet?). I usually take the kitten and put them in the litter box – so they understand it, feel it, etc.

If your "safe" room is a bedroom, all the better because then your kitten can sleep with a member of the family – an excellent bond is created. Of course, don't plan on a ton of sleep, unless you are a heavy sleeper - Charlie liked to play a lot at 3AM!

In fact, depending on the time of day you bring your kitty home, you want to set aside about 20-30 minutes before YOUR bedtime to play with your kitten – that way s/he will crash and be fast asleep by the time you fall asleep.

There is no need to rush the first few hours that the kitten is in your home. Spend a lot of time playing and bonding during this first week. If you are patient with your new kitten, the transition will be smooth! Sometimes a kitten is ready to explore the new home within a few hours (i.e., Charlie)!

Depending on the confidence and curiosity of your kitten, you can open the door of this room either a few days, a week or two weeks after s/he has been in there. Let your kitty decide to venture out and explore the rest of the home- when s/he feels ready. Of course, if you have a resident kitty or if you have other resident pets, then this venturing out might not be an easy process.

It is best to bring your kitten home on the weekend or when you can take a few days off of work, so that you can spend a lot of time with your kitten. After the first few days, if you need to go to work, it would be best to close your kitten off in the safe room until the kitten is old enough where s/he will not harm herself or himself. There would be nothing worse than coming home to an injured kitten!

Exploring Your Home

Your kitten will explore your home and start to play and get to know his or her new family and surroundings. A string, cat wand toy or another kind of cat toy is a great way to interact with your new kitten during this time and heck, any time!

If there is a behavior in your kitten that you do not like you might redirect its attention by moving it somewhere else and rewarding the new behavior. Or, if your kitten is jumping on your countertops and you do not want your kitten on your counters, an easy way to deter that behavior is by buying a water spray bottle and spraying your kitten with water when they jump on the counters. They will soon learn that, in order to avoid the spritz of water, they have to avoid the counters. This does not make your kitten scared of water, however, as it is the action of the spray that they don't like. You're using water to spray because it's safe for them.

Another option includes putting 20 pennies in an aluminum drink can and then taping (with duct tape or something similar) the lid so the pennies don't fall out (the Miller Lite Aluminum Cans with screw tops are PERFECT for this). When you see your kitten doing something you disapprove of—just shake the can with the pennies. Kittens and cats do not like that sound! The sound of the pennies on the aluminum will really discourage them from continuing their misbehavior.

If you have potted plants that your kitten will not avoid – consider buying decorative bark or rock that will not interest them as much as that loose, rich soil. You can also put aluminum foil over the dirt – they don't care for the feel of the aluminum under their paws.

Kitten Safety in Your Home

Remember to check lower cabinets, dishwashers, clothes washers and dryers before closing, just in case your kitten decides it would be a nice place to hide, nap or play in one of those locations. Keep doors to the dishwasher, the washing machine, the clothes dryer and the chest-type freezer closed at all times except for when you are standing there. Never leave a door open even for a moment as kittens are quick and can easily hide inside. You might not miss them at first and they could really get in trouble. A suggestion about the clothes dryer: always stand by it a few moments after it is started and listen for any bumping. Better safe than sorry.

Trigg loved my clothes dryer when he first arrived – as seen in the photo. Especially because I have those dryer balls that make fun sounds. However, I quickly discouraged his interest in the dryer by throwing the clothes from the washer quickly in the dryer – he didn't like being in the way!

Inform family and guests to watch the small opening where door hinges are and the front/outside of doors as they open and close them to avoid little kitten's paws and tails getting caught (Rags' tail always had a little crook at the end of it because it was shut in a door at one point). Remind visitors that your kitten is an indoor pet, and to not let them outside. A collar with a bell on it is a good idea both so you know if your kitten is under-foot, as well as where s/he is when near doors. They can be very sneaky! Just make sure it is a "break-away" style so the kitten does not catch him/herself on something and choke.

Be careful when raising or lowering recliner chairs and power beds as kittens can often play underneath and can be hurt by the metal working parts.

Also always check under quilts or throws on beds and couches before sitting on them as kitties like to burrow in a warm nest to sleep. Common sense and caution will make your home a safe and loving environment for your new baby kittens.

Summary of Things to Watch Out For:

- Washing Machines
- Clothes dryers
- Refrigerator or freezer doors
- Hot oven doors
- Hot stovetop burners (an empty burner that has just been turned off) - If your cat or kitten gets near the stovetop, a good suggestion is to keep a large tea kettle with water in it and place it on the still-hot burner until it has cooled off.
- RECLINERS and/or RECLINER-ROCKERS
- Unprotected screens in windows

If you have young children, you will want to encourage them to calmly greet the new kitten and refrain from loud noises and extreme actions of excitement. Of course, this can be hard because your children are excited and want to interact with their new baby kitten.

Just remind them of a time when they were scared or apprehensive and it is best if they have a cool, calm, collected approach to keep kitty from being startled by unfamiliar sounds. Think of it as introducing your children to an infant. Soon the kitten and your children will be best of friends – your kitten might become your child's next doll – being dressed up in clothes and strolled around in a stroller.

Teach children how to hold a Ragdoll, supporting them properly under their chest and the kitten's bottom, as Ragdolls are quite floppy! And let them know to put the kitty down carefully if s/he wants down. Teach your children to leave a sleeping baby kitten alone as this is when kittens grow and develop, s/he can be in deep sleep and shouldn't be disturbed too often at nap time. If your kitty is awakened a lot from much needed naps s/he may resort to sleeping where s/he won't be bothered as easily, like under beds or out of sight. Kittens sleep over 85 percent of each day when young, just like little human babies!

Socializing Your Kitten

Socialize your kitten by handling it (this is more important for a not-so-confident kitten). Encourage visitors that aren't scared of kittens to hold, play and touch your kitten, so that your new pet can get used to strangers and how other people might interact with them. This also helps them adapt to change. No matter where you are in life – just out of college, an empty nester or about to have children – helping to socialize your kitten for your lifestyle will make your life easier in the long run.

Touch your kitten everywhere! They should be used to you touching their paws, face, legs, tail, belly, you name it. One of the great benefits of getting a cat from the kitten stage is that you can "train" it to accept being touched by you and anyone else anywhere on its body. This makes for much easier vet visits in the future and your vet will thank you.

Holding Your Kitten

When it comes to handling your kitten, you want to hold them so that you don't scrunch any of their limbs. My cousin was sweet enough to send me photos of her holding her sweet, Huck, so could see the various styles.

When walking around with a kitten in your arms, it's best to do like they do at the cat shows. They run their hand up under-

neath the cat from back to front, with the weight of the cat weighing mostly on their forearm and open palm underneath the chest/ribs. Their legs are actually on each side of your forearm. I've seen many folks walk around with their kitties being carried that way while they are doing other things with their other hand/arm. It's amazing to watch.

Vets sometimes do this at the vet's office. That way, the entire length of the cat's body is supported. Of course, when Ragdolls get to be 15 to 20 pounds or more, it's much harder carrying them around.

You might want to pick up kittens by gently supporting underneath their rib cage with one hand and cupping your other hand around their rumps. As you get them up close to your body or your chest, move that hand to support their backs while still holding them by their rumps. It's much like holding a baby when burping them.

I also like to hold my cats like a baby in both arms, with their belly up. Some kittens come already doing this, whereas others have to learn to trust you holding them that way. Many Ragdolls love the belly-up thing, but there are many that do NOT. Those are the ones you carry with their undersides supported on your lower arm or else in the burping position.

Keep in mind that every cat is different, and you just want to make sure that you hold them so that they are always comfortable.

What it boils down to is if your kitten is comfortable – not squirming in your arms or complaining about being there – then you are doing it right. See more photos of how to hold a cat (http://bit.ly/Olurse) and how to hold a kitten (http://bit.ly/T6l2WG) on the site.

Chapter 3

Ragdoll Kitten's Diet, Food and Water Bowls, Treats

Food recommendations, such as what to feed your kitty and when, should come from your breeder and then ultimately from your vet. There is a great cat resource online written by a California veterinarian, Lisa A. Pierson, DVM, that addresses the dangers of a dry food diet (http://catinfo.org/). Decisions about what to feed your cat, which brand of food and what type of food are something that you will have to come to terms with based on your budget, your lifestyle, your living situation and your vet's recommendation (and whether or not you trust your vet or if you think s/he is being paid by the large pet food companies to sell product). You might also find this page on Liz Eastwood's blog, The Natural Cat Care Blog – The Best Canned Cat Foods (http://bit.ly/RHdyfW), helpful.

Keep in mind that the recommended food quantities on pet food containers are based on the amount needed by active cats living in multiple cat households and the amount needed by sedentary, neutered or spayed cats is often much lower. You'll want to seek your veterinarian's advice as to the type and amount of food to feed your cat.

Remember that cats in the wild eat many small meals per day and smaller meals more frequently might help you avoid problems with obesity later on.

Be sure to monitor eating habits in the first week. You'll want to continue the food regime that the breeder or your vet recommends. If you are switching their food, you have to do it slowly to prevent stress and diarrhea.

So no matter if you want to switch your kitty from the food the breeder was feeding to something else or not, be sure to have some of the food on hand that the breeder was feeding your kitten. They will recognize the smell and eat it. If you decide to feed a different brand, gradually mix it up to 50/50 with your kitten's previous brand for a week before switching over to the new brand. This way, your kitten's body can adapt to a different diet. Be sure the brand you switch to has low or no by-products and is high in protein for the best health of your kitten, especially in the first year of growth.

If you have a multiple cat household, you might eventually consider setting up several feeding stations throughout your home – that way cats can avoid or greet the cats they want to without fighting and more importantly, without spraying! It will totally depend on your situation though; Charlie and Trigg have one feeding station – in the kitchen and eat peacefully next to one another.

A water bowl is essential as well – especially if you are only feeding your kitten dry food. You will want to get something sturdy and deep. Some kittens like to play in the water and if it's sturdy, then they cannot tip it over, so less clean up for you.

You might consider having at least two water bowls, possibly in different areas. That way, if one was spilled, the kitten would have access to another water bowl.

Food and Water Bowls

There are a lot of options when it comes to food and water bowls for kitties. Plastic food bowls tends to hold bacteria and are also known to cause feline acne. I do love, ModaPet bowls that are made from plastic – Charlie does not get acne from everyday use of these, but Trigg does. However, I have found that Trigg doesn't get acne if I feed one meal a day in those bowls – so that's what we do! So you may want to choose a metal bowl or a ceramic bowl instead and be sure that it is dishwasher-safe to make your life easier. I love this heart shaped bowl – but as of right now, it's only available for shipment in Europe.

If your kitty is on an all wet food diet, you will be surprised to learn that they don't drink much water. In fact, Charlie and Trigg don't even have a water bowl, because they never drink water. You can learn more about how wet food gives them the moisture that they need in their diet when you read Dr. Lisa Pierson's Cat Info Site (http://catinfo.org/).

If you do have a water dish, you might consider dropping a few cubes of ice into their water bowl every day. Many cats love playing with the ice until it melts (make certain the kitty is there at the bowl when you drop in the ice cubes). Then, when they are done playing, you can refill the water bowl(s) with fresh water.

Moreover, when they are teething, cold things always seem to help little gums as the teeth are coming in. So the trick really is for them to get the chips into their mouths. You want to make sure you are there for safety's sake - never leave the area until their chips/cubes are completely melted.

Another option for water drinking is to get a cat water fountain – Keith Davitt makes custom ones that are really neat.

There is a neat product on the market called the Neater Feeder. It is a mess-proof pet feeder. For a kitten, the size might be too big, but for an adult cat it works well – it is a plastic outer shell with two stainless steel bowls. Anything that the cat drops out of the two stainless steel bowls will drop in to the plastic outer shell, eliminating a lot of clean up on your end. You can see our review of the Neater Feeder here (http://bit.ly/ VGKxTi).

I prefer to use individual bowls because that works for us – but there are different products on the market depending on what you're looking for. Check out the "Eat" portion on the site, where I feature bowls and food that we're reviewing for ideas of what may work for you.

Treats

At this point, I only recommend a few treats and those are Whole Life Pet Products' cat treats (which can also be fed to dogs), Honest Kitchen's Wishes as well as Eden Foods' Bonito Flakes which

The Whole Life Pet Products' cat treats are freeze dried versions of the muscle of an animal – so for example, their Chicken is literally freeze dried chicken breast – pure and simple and natural. They have recently come out with an Organic treat line. You can also request a free sample to make sure that your kitty likes the treats before you buy a big bag of them. Read our reviews and see our video review here (http://bit.ly/Up6PLp)

(we have reviewed a lot of flavors – so just click on each link of the flavor you're interested in).

Honest Kitchen's Wishes are freeze dried 100% human-grade, wild caught Icelandic Haddock. These come in giant pieces that can be broken into smaller bits, but can be eaten as a whole piece – and the challenge of eating the big piece is a good exercise for your kitty. Available in 2 oz. Read our review and see our video review here (http://bit.ly/QQoYel).

Eden Foods' Bonito Flakes are shaved Bonito flakes that are tested safe for human consumption. You can buy bonito flakes at major pet retailers, but they are usually not tested for human consumption – mercury and other nuclear levels in fish are something to be aware of! Read our review and see our video review here (http://bit.ly/SCK2ZΛ).

Treats with Interactive Toys and Hunting Games

I love, love, love interactive toys because they decrease mental stagnation and prevent behavior problems which result from boredom in your cat. They also bring out the instinctual nature of your cat to hunt for their food. The Nina Ottosson's Interactive treat puzzles are excellent for this. We have tried out the Dog Spinny and the Dog Brick Game. There are different levels, so you want to start with level one, which in our case was the Dog Spinny.

Another option is the Aïkiou Stimulo Cat Feeding Station and Activity Center. You can see Charlie mastering it in this video (http://bit.ly/VGKUx8).

These games are made from plastic. I prefer the plastic ones because they are dishwasher-safe and easily cleaned. Again, though you need to watch your kitty and make sure s/he is not developing feline acne.

Cat Trees

A question I get often on the site is what kind of cat trees I recommend. I do have a page on the site where you can see some of the great cool cat trees on the market (http://bit.ly/PG63Cg).

The closest we have come to reviewing a cat tree is a product where you build a tower of boxes – they're called Catty Stacks. Catty Stacks are corrugated cardboard cubes that connect to one another and you can put them in any combination that you can think of. You can buy them in different sets and in different colors to really have some fun. Here is a video that shows you what Catty Stacks is all about (http://bit.ly/Q2abie). You can learn more about them by reading our Catty Stacks review (http://bit.ly/QQpkBD) on the site.

Homemade Foraging Toys

You can also make a homemade toy by using a plastic beverage bottle – make sure you have run it through the dishwasher and make sure to clean the cap too (you could always use an empty plastic peanut butter container too). You then want to cut holes in the sides of the bottle large enough for the treats to fall through then stick the treats into the bottle through the human mouth opening and then screw on the lid. If you put it on the floor, then your kitty will start knocking it around trying to figure out how to get to the treats (that is, of course, if they like the treats you put inside). A foraging toy such as this one can keep them entertained for hours and would be ideal if you are gone all day because it will keep your kitty busy until you return.

You can also make homemade puzzle feeders where you cut a hole in a cardboard box and the cat has to paw their food out of the box.

You might even want to hide food or treats in different places throughout your house so that your kitten has to "hunt" for his or her food.

My vet suggests throwing their treats across the room so that they get exercise chasing after them!

Chapter 4

Recommended Scratchers, Toys and Beds

Starting your kitten out with the right scratchers, toys and beds will hopefully avoid destruction of your furniture for years to come.

Cats aren't vindictive. They don't set out to scratch furniture or drapes to cost you more money; they do it because they do not have the appropriate thing to scratch on. Cats have an instinctual nature to scratch because it is a marking behavior – they have special glands on their paws that release their scent and therefore when they scratch, they deposit that scent on the area where they are scratching – and consequently it becomes an area they want to return to – think, "MINE!"

I DO NOT recommend ANY scratcher for your cat that has carpet on it. Allowing your cat to use a scratcher that is covered in carpet will only encourage your kitty to scratch carpet that might be on your stairs or in a room, which can be quite costly to replace. Even if you don't have carpet in your apartment or home now, you might move and that could change in 10 years, so it's better to be safe than sorry. You want your kitty to know that carpet is off limits; therefore it is best to choose scratchers that have cardboard or sisal. The exception to the rule here would be someone that hates carpet and does not and will not ever have it in their home for the duration of the cat's life.

Most cats prefer to scratch either horizontally or vertically; they also usually have a preferred scratching material. Since your kitten is learning what s/he likes, you will want to provide variety. If after you've tested a variety, and your kitty favors one over the other – you can always donate the scratcher s/he doesn't use to a local animal shelter. You may find, however, that your kitty will use both, as mine do.

I recommend both an upright scratcher, such as TopCat Products' Sisal Scratching Posts and also a horizontal scratcher, such as the Brawny Cat Big Baby Lounger - it's a bed and scratcher in one. You can read the product review we did on the TopCat Products' scratching post, if you would like further information about it. Or read our review of the Brawny Cat Big Baby (http://bit.ly/SIviny).

When you start out with a kitten, rather than an older cat that has established scratching habits, you have the opportunity to teach your kitten where it is OK to scratch.

So, for example, when Charlie, as a kitten, would go for the corner of my bed skirt as a great place to scratch, I would say, "No!" and then pick him up and take him over to his Bergan Turbo Scratcher and put him on that for scratching. The great thing about the Bergan Turbo Scratcher is that the corrugated cardboard portion is replaceable so you can remove it, flip it over to get the use out of the other side and then order replacements.

Now, at 3 years of age, he goes to that Bergan Turbo Scratcher and scratches away! The Bergan Turbo Scratcher also makes for a phenomenal toy that your kitty will play with for the rest of its life. See Charlie playing with his Bergan Turbo Track at 2.5 years old (http://bit.ly/VsV2ex)!

Very young kittens (less than 3 months old) and older cats do not respond as much or at all to catnip. In fact, 10-30% of all cats do not respond to catnip at any age. This is due to genetics – reactions to catnip are hereditary – so just ask your breeder if your kitten's parents respond to catnip!

In other words, the way that I trained Charlie to use the Turbo Scratcher (or corrugated cardboard) instead of my bed skirt was by rewarding him with praise (I have a tendency to use a high pitched voice that cats bring out in me to praise them) and pets when he did what I wanted. I do not believe in punishing, swatting, slapping or hitting your cat – I simply redirected the undesired behavior he was displaying. Such a tactic is non-violent and will make your kitty love you all the more.

They will learn and do what you want them to do because of the treats or positive attention you give to them when they do what you want. You can also use treats – think Whole Life treats again. Of course, most scratchers come with catnip that you can sprinkle into the corrugated cardboard or that you can rub on the sisal post. Since kittens usually cannot smell catnip until they are older, this doesn't always work. So you

can also use toys like the Neko Flies or strings to encourage your cat to just check out the scratcher. This is what we did with Charlie and Trigg to encourage them to use and explore the feeling of the TopCat Sisal Posts.

I just took the Neko Flies cat wand and would hover it over the top of the post and they wanted to get to it badly enough that they would climb the pole!

For a kitten, when you provide play with a scratcher – it not only becomes a two-in-one toy, but also ends up being a great way to encourage them to scratch on something different – this is true with the Bergan Turbo Scratcher.

A scratcher and cat bed that I cannot get Trigg off of is the Petstages Snuggle Scratch and Rest. It is also made of corrugated cardboard, but it shaped like a bowl, so it's easy for them to feel cozy in it! You can see more of Trigg in it in this video (http://bit.ly/RHelgZ).

The Sleepypod Crater Dot is the bed that sits right next to the Petstages Snuggle Scratch and Rest in our home. The cats love it. It has the same concept as the Petstages Snuggle Scratch and Rest in that it is designed much like a bowl and contours to their body. See our video of it here (http://bit.ly/Slvqne).

Another great scratcher that is new as of 2012 is the kittyblock. It is a cube made of corrugated cardboard that has a square cut-out in the center, so they can go on top or inside. Check out the photo of Charlie on one – you can tell it is a nice size. Here is our arrival video of the kittyblock (http://bit.ly/Rjro6b) which will show you more of it and you can see how the cats interact with it.

Imperial Cat makes all different shapes and sizes of corrugated cat scratchers. Charlie and Trigg have product tested several of their styles and shapes and love them all. They are immediately attracted to them and usually I can find one of them laying on one of their scratchers. We reviewed the Imperial Cat Zen Lounger and more. Here's a video of it too (http://bit.ly/R4s9zF).

Whatever scratchers you decide to buy – be sure that they are sturdy (cats are easily discouraged from a non-sturdy object) and are made of materials that cats prefer such as cardboard, natural wood or sisal rope.

All the scratchers I have mentioned above also have replacement options – so in other words, when your kitty has used the scratcher to the point where it needs replacing – you can buy a replacement pad or pole or just another one from any of these companies.

Placement of the Scratcher

It is important to place the scratcher close to where s/he is inclined to scratch – this can be next to a window, near a sleeping area or another favorite area. I noticed when Charlie was a kitten that he always liked to scratch when he woke up from a nap, so I typically had a scratcher near wherever he slept.

Believe me, once their scent is on that scratcher, they will not care where you move it – they will find it and use it. For example, Charlie's Turbo Scratcher used to be in the master bedroom, but since I got sick of hearing the ball roll around the Turbo Scratcher at 3AM, I moved it to the guest bedroom and that's where he uses it.

Now that he is older, he doesn't play at 3AM, so when we have house guests, I simply move the scratcher back in my room and he always knows where it is! He now plays at 6AM!

Also, to discourage 3AM play on the Turbo Scratcher, simply turn it upside down and slide it underneath a dresser or a sofa for the night. Just remember to turn it upright early the next morning or else your kitty will go searching for it.

Recommended Toys

Toys are an important part in the bonding process with your new kitten but also an important part in their overall health and well-being. An enriched environment for your kitty can provide increased activity, decrease in mental stagnation and can even end up preventing behavior problems.

Rule #1! Your hands and feet are not toys! Substitute any biting of hands or feet with a toy. When we first got Charlie, Bill (boyfriend) played with Charlie with his fingers and when I brought Charlie to the vet a few days later, he went after the vet's fingers! So embarrassing, especially when she said, "I see someone has been playing with Charlie with their fingers!" Here's a popular video on YouTube of Bill being guilty of that (http://bit.ly/QBHWqA).

Instead, here are some great toys to consider buying for your new kitten that s/he will also enjoy as an adult cat.

Interactive Toys

Interactive toys allow your kitty to stalk, catch and play. I recommend Neko Flies which are fantastic cat wand toys, the Undercover Mouse, the PetStages Cuddle Coil and any of the Nina Ottosson's Interactive treat puzzles – we've tried out the Dog Spinny and the Dog Brick so far. Both are great.

I cover the Nina Ottosson's Interactive treat puzzles as well as the Aïkiou Stimulo Cat Feeding Station and Activity Center in Chapter 3, and in an effort not to be repetitive, I won't talk about them here. Of course, if you would like to read our product reviews on her Dog Spinny and the Dog Brick which are on Floppycats.com, you're more than welcome to do so.

Neko Flies

Neko Flies are cat wand toys – of the fishing type variety. They remind me much of fly fishing.

We have done product reviews on these as well. Ellen, the owner and creator of these was sick and tired of cat wand toys that easily fall apart – and believe me, we have gotten our fair share of products to test that have done exactly that! So when I recommend these, I do whole heartedly. They are a hit with Caymus, Murphy, Charlie and Trigg as well as a friend of mine's two domestic short hair cats. I have not tested them on other Ragdolls, but the 4 I have all love them as well as my friend's rescue cats! And it is an instantaneous love.

You can buy the wand and attachments separately, so that they always have a new attachment to play with.

Another wand toy that is quite popular and supported heavily by Jackson Galaxy host of Animal Planet's My Cat from Hell is Da Bird. I have never used it, but have heard great things about it, so thought I would include it.

Undercover Mouse

My mom's sister adopted a Ragdoll from Sweden named Prince William. A friend of my Aunt's sent her the Undercover Mouse toy and Prince William would play with it for hours.

As the name of the product suggests, there is an undercover "mouse" that moves around under the yellow nylon skirt. This interactive cat toy brings out the hunter/predator skills in your kitty – just watch the videos on our You-Tube channel to see how Charlie and Trigg got into it (http://bit.ly/WwzGeh).

So I know five Ragdoll cats who love this thing! It also has various attachments that you can buy afterwards.

Petstages Cat Cuddle Coil

The Petstages Cuddle Coil is a polka-dot popup play tunnel – usually found at any large pet store and also online. Kitties love the protection and comfort that it provides. It's made of cuddly-soft padded nylon material that encases sturdy coil for comfort and support. The back is enclosed for added security and privacy.

I don't know what it is about the Petstages Cuddle Coil but it seems that every cat likes these – at least every cat I have seen interact with it!

Caymus (pictured with it) is eight years-old and he still plays in the one my mom got him as a kitten! He definitely sticks out the back end, but he loves it – totally puts him in a good mood and makes him a purring machine. See a video of Caymus playing in it (http://bit.ly/PG6VXk).

Catnip Toys

Hands down, without question, you should buy a Yeowww! Catnip Banana. It is shaped like a banana – the outside is a yellow canvas like material and the banana is stuffed with 100% pure organic catnip. It will last for years and 99% of the time your cat will love it and play with it daily.

My mom first discovered these when Rags was 15 years old and she put one in his stocking at Christmas. It was a hit thereafter. Rags never played with toys past the first 15 minutes, but the Yeowww! Catnip Banana was one that he returned to over and over again.

You might just want to buy one to start out with and then move onto buying them in bulk as I do now. Every time a friend gets a kitten or their cat has a birthday, they get a Yeowww! Catnip Banana from me. Watch a video compilation of Caymus, Murphy, Rags, Charlie and Trigg all playing with Yeowww! Catnip Toys (http://bit.ly/QZ5Vlw).

Additionally, you'll want to find out what the breeder has been using for toys and see what she or he suggests for your new kitty. For example, there are certain toys your kitty will be naturally attracted to that the breeder already has been using and s/he can tell you which toys your kitty likes best – if she doesn't know the names of them, have her send you a photo to see if you can find them at the local pet store.

If you have dogs or small children that might eat cat toys avoid the toys with plastic centers as they are small and can be dangerous to ingest and they can be a child choking hazard. If you have little children, be sure all toys for your kitty are child safe too. For example, it might be a good idea to have all cloth type cat toys around kids and dogs (like the Yeowww! Catnip Banana).

If it is a stuffed toy and your kitty has the stuffing pulling out, throw away the toy so your kitty does not eat the stuffing – this is what I like about the Yeowww! Catnip Banana – it has no polyfill – it is stuffed with 100% pure catnip.

The crunchy foil balls are also popular with kittens. My mom's 8-year old, Murphy, still enjoys them quite a bit – hauls them around the house in his mouth meowing while he walks. Of course, you can make something similar by just wadding up a sheet of foil paper into a ball.

Great free toys include bottle caps from plastic bottles – I like to throw them across the room and the cats love to chase them and bat at them. These could be a choking hazard for a small child or a dog, though.

Another cheap toy you can make is to take two or three cable ties (these can be purchased in bright, vivid colors) and then loop them together like a paper chain. Remember to snip off the pointed ends. These toys go scooting across the floor and the cats love them. They can also be carried around in their mouths and taken to another area for play. Just remember to make the loops large enough that they cannot swallow them. You can get the 13 or 14 inch lengths and purchase these cable ties at any home improvement store in a bag of 100. They're cheap entertainment for both kittens and older cats alike – heck, you might already have these in your home anyway.

I also make this homemade toy with a wire dry cleaner hanger and the end of a check book. Here is a video of Charlie and Trigg playing with said toy (http://bit.ly/TbofcV).

Boxes and Bags

Both kittens and cats love to play in boxes and paper bags – just make sure the bags aren't plastic – the brown paper ones from the grocery store are best because they usually don't have handles. Handles can wrap around a kitten's neck and if they cannot get out of it, they can be strangled to death – especially if they are not being supervised. So be sure not to have one that has handles or that could cause suffocation.

Cat Beds

You might want to get a bed for your new kitty – Charlie and Trigg sometimes prefer to sleep on the couch or on a chair – but those items might be off limits in your household.

Kitties like empty boxes with a small towel in the bottom of them (which can be removed for cleaning) or you can always buy a round cat bed. Kitties love to sleep in round beds. I recommend the Alpha Pooch Siesta Bowl – it comes in a brown and natural.

As I mentioned earlier, the Sleepypod Crater Dot is a favorite in our house.

Some of the scratchers I've already mentioned in this eBook also serve as cat beds - Petstages Snuggle Scratch and Rest, Imperial Cat Zen Lounger and the Brawny Cat Big Baby Lounger.

Chapter 5

Carriers and Your First Vet Visits

The reason I included "carriers" with the vet visit here is because it is very important to bring your kitty to the vet in a carrier. As much as you just want to hold that little bundle of fur, it is not only better for your kitty but also for you to know that your kitty is protected and cannot leap out of your arms into the parking lot or onto a busy street.

Moreover, when a kitty gets scared they can sometimes have a reaction you won't expect and they can end up injuring you trying to get out of your arms.

Your vet will have smells, sounds and sights that your kitty isn't used to, as well as other strange dogs and/or cats.

So the proper pet carrier can give your kitty the safe haven s/he needs while on his or her first trip to the vet and every subsequent visit. Plus the carrier will more than likely smell like your home, so your kitty will associate it with love and protection. Reducing your young kitten's exposure to other cats will decrease their stress as well as their exposure to illness, which is another reason to have a great carrier. In fact, keeping them in the carrier the entire time they are at the vet is even better.

If the breeder is shipping the kitten to you, then your kitten will come in a carrier when you pick it up from the airport – and you will have already paid for the cost of the carrier and the shipping charges of the cat. So if you already have a carrier in mind, you could certainly ask your breeder if you can have one shipped to them so that your kitty comes home in the carrier you want (it will have to meet airline regulations though). If you go to pick up your kitten, then you will want to bring a carrier with you. If you go to a pet store to get a carrier, be sure to get a carrier that your kitten can grow into to save you money in the long run. You will want a carrier large enough for a 25 lb. animal.

I like any carrier that allows you to take off the top – in other words, one like the Sleepypod or most of the Petmate Pet Carriers (I like their Kennel Cab Fashion Carrier) will work for this purpose. That way the vet can unscrew the top of the carrier (or in the Sleepypod's case unzip the top), so that the vet will have full access to the kitty. The Sleepypod has a weight limit of 15 lbs, though – so just be aware that your kitty may grow out of it.

Likewise, let your vet do all of the handling of your kitten. The vet is used to a certain amount of anxiety in cats and kittens and can easily modify their approach depending on the reaction of the kitty.

Many people keep their cat carrier in an area where the kitten or cat can use it as an alternate bed (this is the idea behind the Sleepypod – when not used as a carrier, it is a stylish bed and looks like a fancy round bed when the top is zipped off).

To make a plastic carrier into a bed - remove the door and keep a towel or soft padding inside and it will be a place for naps and play. This will make the carrier a less stressful place to be placed in when transporting to and from the vet as well.

Veterinarians

You want to set up an appointment to see your local veterinarian shortly after your kitten comes home as recommended in Chapter 1.

If you don't have a vet, you'll want to ask your friends or neighbors with animals if they will recommend a vet for you. Ideally one closer to home is great because if there is an emergency, it will not take a long time to get your kitten into the office.

Once you have a vet lined up you will want to bring your new kitty to see them. In fact, if you know the date that you will be bringing your new kitty home; you should go ahead and schedule a vet appointment for that day or the following day. For example, I got Charlie on a Thursday and he met my vet the next day. I got Trigg on a Saturday and he met the vet on Monday (and didn't meet Charlie until he was cleared from the vet – of course, they came from the same cattery, but you can never be too sure and I didn't want to jeopardize either one of them).

Bringing a new animal into your home is an exciting thing, but if not done properly, the new kitty can cause stress and possibly bring something from their first home into your home. It is better to be safe than sorry!

Your breeder will most likely have already taken your kitten to the vet for their first round of shots and will tell you when the next round of shots are due. Depending on your breeder and your vet, you might not give your kitten all vaccines that your breeder recommends or that your vet recommends.

Your breeder will most likely send home a health record and sometimes will include the stickers from the vaccines administered to your kitten on that health record. The stickers are important because that way your vet can see the brand, lot number and expiration date from the labels.

In choosing which vaccines, flea treatments and heartworm treatments your kitten/cat should receive, you will need to know the benefits and risks of both. This is not something I can recommend or not recommend. It is a personal decision based on your lifestyle, your beliefs and where you live. You'll want to get a full understanding from your vet as to the benefits and side effects of the vaccines. A well-respected holistic veterinarian, Jean Hofve, has an excellent website that addresses a lot of cat health related questions called, Little Big Cat. She also has a page on vaccinations in cats (http://bit.ly/R4suT0) and the dangers involved in the over-vaccination of kitties which might give you more insight and help you in your decision as to which vaccines to give your kitty.

More than likely your vet will have a recommended kitten vaccination schedule. There might be vaccinations required within the city/county/state where you live as well. Your vet will know this information.

There's always a chance that your kitty could get sick or could come to you sick, so it's important to be aware of these symptoms of a sick cat, in case that were to happen.

Some symptoms of a sick cat include:

- decrease in appetite
- diarrhea
- vomiting
- dull hair coat
- listlessness
- weight loss
- red, watery eyes

- sneezing
- nasal discharge
- straining when urinating or defecating
- frequent trips to the litter box
- bloody urine
- changes in litter box habits

Vet Costs

I checked with my vet, KC Cat Clinic in Kansas City, MO, USA for these figures – obviously these are going to vary by where you live and what the cost of living is. Also, please be aware that KC Cat Clinic's prices include a lot of doctor time talking about lifestyles and behavior things to look out for – this isn't only about vaccinating kittens.

Breeders usually do the first round of vaccines for your kitten and this is based on the breeder's opinion on what vaccines are necessary. Some breeders administer the vaccines themselves whereas others bring their kittens to the vet to have them done

These are current as of September 2012.

- **1st year** - around $550.00 for a healthy kitten. This does not include Feline Leukemia, FIV testing, spay or neuter (many breeders will send you your kitten already spayed or neutered and I prefer breeders that do this because it shows their responsibility in keeping the breed strong) which runs about $55. KC Cat Clinic spaces out their vaccines over a 16 week period which is recommended by American Association of Feline Practitioners. Of course, if they see something they are concerned about, like a skin issue, then the cost for the 1st year could go up depending on what it is.

Cat Health Insurance

Depending on where you live in the world, you may be interested in getting cat health insurance. Of course, if you've read my site, then you know that my Rags was diagnosed with lymphoma at the age of 16 and went through chemotherapy treatments and what not. We did not have cat health insurance and therefore, it was a very expensive endeavor. Of course, there is no guarantee that you will know what, if anything will happen to your kitten during its lifetime.

Because of this and because there are limitations to cat health insurance policies in certain areas, you might consider setting aside the amount you would normally pay for a premium and setting up an additional bank account just for your cat. There's really no way to guess if anything will happen to your kitty and by having it in a separate account – you can either spend it if you need to or use it for another reason if you don't need to spend it on your kitty.

KC Cat Clinic recommends putting aside $50/month per cat in a separate savings or money market account. That way if anything happens in their life time, you can use the money from that account. If your cat remains healthy, then you've got a great savings account set up.

Chapter 6

Nail Trimming and Grooming

Nail Trimming

Nail trimming from a young age is important. I have heard so many stories of people that cannot clip their cat's nails and therefore have to haul them to the vet to have it done there. It's best to get them used to it (and you too) as a kitten, so that it's an easy process for the remainder of their life.

The part of the nail that you want to trim is only the tiny sharp white tips- not back to the pink quick! Cats have five nails/claws in the front, including the dewclaw, and usually only four in the back.

To get your kitten used to nail grooming, handle their paws often when grooming and petting – you also want to spread their toes and push on their pads lightly, so they get used to it. If your kitty is not happy or compliant, try doing just one foot at a time or give extra love and a snack afterwards, to help this become a more positive experience. It will get easier in time.

Some kitties have ticklish back feet so be patient in your grooming so s/he does not

feel like it is a negative experience – in fact, when I started trimming Charlie and Trigg's nails, I usually tried to catch them right after a nap so that they were still sort of out of it from the nap and not nearly as responsive as they would be right before playing.

Front claws will probably need trimming every three to four weeks. Back feet may only need to be trimmed every two or more months or so, as they usually wear differently than the front feet – back claws do not get the workout from the scratchers that front claws do.

I recommend small scissors made for kitties (like the ones pictured). Trimming their nails is an important part of the bonding process, not to mention an important part in making sure your skin isn't accidentally clawed when they are sitting on your lap and kneading. Sharp nails can hurt – even when your kitten doesn't mean to use them intentionally!

The JW Pet Company GripSoft Nail Clipper for Pets, Small (pictured) work just fine.

To know how to trim their nails properly, have the vet show you on your first visit, so that you can see what part of the nail you want to trim. You can also see the video I made when I trimmed Trigg's nails (http://bit.ly/PYCQUp) with the JW Pet Company GripSoft Nail Clipper for Pets, Small

It is very important that you do this from the beginning so that your cat gets used to the feeling of you extending their claws out to cut them as well as the compression of the scissor cutting down on their claws.

Grooming

When Rags got old, he didn't take care of his coat and stopped grooming as often; as a result he got mats. Thank goodness that I got him when I was a little girl and as a result he was often brushed with every doll brush I ever owned.

The point is – by the time he was an old guy, he was used to being brushed.

It's a good idea to brush or comb your kitten once a week or even every day as it not only helps to keep their coat soft and clean, it also creates a great bonding experience between you and your cat. It also allows your cat to become used to being touched anywhere (which is fantastic for future vet visits) and lets you get to know your kitty's body – so that you can watch out for scratches and injuries.

Some great brushes and combs that we have reviewed:

- JW Pet Slicker Brush
- JW Pet Comb
- JW Pet Shedding Blade
- Rakom Cat Grooming Tool

As far as which brush to get, ask your breeder what s/he has used. Charlie and Trigg hate being brushed, so they only like the Rakom Cat Grooming Tool and the Tangle Teezer – a human brush I found at CVS.

Most Ragdolls, though, do not have fur that tangles and it is relatively mat-free. Their coats are usually medium to long and have a soft, silky texture. If you live in an area where there are four seasons, then your Ragdoll may shed more fur in the spring, for example, as they de-shed to their summer coat and get rid of their winter one.

If for some reason your kitten needs a bath to clean a dirty bottom or something along those lines, then I recommend having a bottle of shampoo/conditioner on hand like the Pet Naturals of Vermont's CLEAN Shampoo and Conditioner in one on hand. CLEAN is an all-natural 2-in-1 shampoo + conditioner. It's free of fillers, thickeners, harsh additives, oils, lanolins, and silicones and is biodegradable. It is also safe for use on puppies, adult dogs and cats! Overall, Ragdolls are good about keeping themselves clean and groomed.

If you, for some reason, need a great grooming system, I recommend Scaredy Cut. Scaredy Cut is a silent and vibration free trimming system that uses high quality barber scissors regulated by attachment guide combs. A set of six guide combs provide regulated cutting from 0.5 inches up to 1.0 inches. Scissor blades are guarded by the attached combs while cutting and the scissor tip is rounded for safety. You can use the Scaredy Cut scissor with the comb attached to gently brush your pet prior to trimming.

Chapter 7

Litter Box

Another benefit of buying a kitten from a breeder is that your kitten will already be trained on how to use a litter box because the mama kitty teaches her kittens about the litter box.

You want to start out with the same litter the kitten was using at the breeder and then potentially move over to another kind of litter based on the recommendation of your vet, or based on what you already use in your household (if you already have other cats).

If you already have another kitty, you will probably want to eventually use the same litter for both cats for convenience sake. For your new kitten, start out with 100% of the breeder litter. In the second week, add half of your preferred brand litter making it a 50-50 mix. In the third week, increase your preferred brand to 75%. By the fourth week, the litter box will have 100% of your preferred brand of litter.

- 1st week – 100% of breeder litter
- 2nd week – 50% of breeder litter; 50% of your current or preferred litter
- 3rd week – 25% of breeder litter; 75% of your current or preferred litter
- 4th week – 100% of your current or preferred litter

Next, you want to consider placement. Of course, the litter box will be placed in the "safe room" from the start and you will probably want to keep it in that room until the kitten is old enough before moving it. If the "safe room" is connected to a bathroom, then that is a great place to put it. I typically grab an old bath mat and stick it under the litter box, so that when the cats get out of the litter box it collects any litter bits that come off their paws and creates an easier cleaning method for me.

You don't want to move your kitten's litter box around frequently. They need to get used to its placement so that, if they get discombobulated in your house, they will always know where their litter box is located.

Of course if you are a one cat household or if you have two new kittens, for example, there's no reason why you cannot have an additional litter box that you want your kitten to transition to outside of the safe room. For example, when I brought Charlie home, his safe room was in my master bedroom/bath. I got sick of the litter box being in my master bath, so I put another in the guest bath and after a few weeks removed the one in the master bath and Charlie used the one in the guest bath instead. Now if guests come, I just move it to the master bath until they leave…Trigg and Charlie have yet to have an accident – knock on wood!

I've read that a laundry room, bathroom or a den are great places for a litter box. My mom has her litter boxes in the basement (this isn't great if you are an out-of-sight-out-of-mind type of person because you can forget that they need to be scooped!) because she has two German Shepherds and dogs are notorious for eating poop out of the litter box!

So she had a carpenter cut out a panel in her 8 panel doors that the cats can use as a cat door. You literally don't even know there's a cat door there! You can see her dog Napa in the photo – she knows where the door is because the cats go in and out of it, but she cannot get through the panel! Here's a video of my mom's cat door (http://bit.ly/Up8HUx).

With a good litter box habit, cats are probably one of the easiest animals to take care of because they do not demand a lot of attention and certainly because they go potty indoors.

I once heard you should have one litter box/per floor/per cat. So in my house, that would be six litter boxes. But I have three - one in my master bath and one on the first floor and one in the basement. I got used to a lot of litter boxes when Rags was going through renal failure (when you have an old cat in renal failure you scoop a lot because they pee a lot) and as a result Trigg and Charlie benefited from my constant cleaning of the litter box.

Since nearly all my litter boxes are by a human toilet, I tend to scoop them as often as I pee – I literally pee and scoop! Makes it easy and keeps it clean and since it is always in my face, it is always clean. It's a good idea to keep your kitty's litter box as clean as possible – think about it – would you want to walk on your old pee or feces to go the bathroom again? EW and YUCK!

You will need a larger litter box like this one from Petco or you could even get a cement mixing tub from a home improvement store (a lot of Ragdoll breeders do this) to accommodate your Ragdoll cat, so even as a little kitten, it won't hurt for them to have a large place to go. The cement mixing tubs are designed for easy mixing and scooping, so they have a curved bottom and no sharp corners inside — perfect for easily scooping litter. They come in different sizes, the small tubs are around 24" x 20" x 6" and cost $6 or $7 and the large tubs measure 24" x 36" x 8" and only cost about $13.

Since your Ragdoll kitten will end up being larger than the average cat, s/he will also produce larger fecal matter, so you will want to make sure you clean the litter pan twice daily. If you think about it, cats have a keener since of smell than humans and they, much like us, wouldn't enjoy walking in their own feces or waste.

A cat on a proper diet of moisture-rich canned food will often pee AT LEAST 3 x/day. That means that one cat with one box will have AT LEAST 21 urinations in that box before you clean his litter box at the end of one week. Therefore it is recommended to scoop AT LEAST daily if not twice daily and then dump the entire contents of the litter box once a week.

I probably dump the entire contents of the litter box and then clean it out with soap and water once a month – I really just watch it and when it gets "nasty" I clean it full force. Since I clean it so regularly on a daily basis, I feel I am able to go longer. It's really up to you – if the litter has a lot of little clumps and smells then change it more often.

If you use a disinfectant to clean the litter box, be sure it is safe for your kitty. Disinfectants that contain phenols and cresols can be lethal to cats as they can absorb them through their paws. Cats are also very allergic to Pine Sol and Antifreeze. My vet suggests chlorine based products or normal bleach mixed at 10% bleach to 90% water. Another good cleaner is 10% vinegar to 90% water.

It is important to consider clumping clay litter for your kitten because, if the litter does not clump, the removal of it is more difficult and leaves remnants in the box for the cat later on. Urine soaks into plastic which is porous – leaving a lasting odor for the life of that box unless you use liners which annoy many cats and really are not necessary if a litter pan is properly maintained.

I recently interviewed Dr. Elsey of Precious Cat Litters, who told me that plastic litter boxes should be changed out (in other words, get rid of the old litter box and buy a brand new one) every year because they absorb the odors of the urine and feces. While you might not be able to smell it, your kitty can and such odors can discourage them from using the litter box.

They do not make commercial litter boxes big enough for large cats, and they do not make any hooded boxes that are even close to being large enough. So a good substitute is to use storage boxes, like ones made by Sterlite or Rubbermaid that you can buy at Wal-mart or Target. Now that Charlie and Trigg are full grown cats, we have moved to storage bins for litter boxes – you can see a video of that here (http://bit.ly/OIwoVI). I spent $5 per storage container.

If you have a hooded litter box, the ammonia odor is trapped in these pans and can really be offensive to your cat (and you!).

I like clumping litter. I ONLY use a clumping litter as all of the NON-clumping litters are very unsanitary (in my opinion) and cause many, many cases of elimination issues. Non-clumping litter allows cats to walk in a litter box that is literally saturated in urine (dry or wet). When urine dries, things are made worse. The only thing that evaporated urine leaves is uric acid/ammonia after the water evaporates. This makes things worse because the uric acid/ammonia is MUCH MORE concentrated.

NO ODOR should be present in a litter box. Use clumping litter so that ALL urine and ALL feces can be removed and there will not be an issue with odor.

Again, I suggest reading more on Dr. Pierson's website - Dr. Pierson's Litter Box Page (http://bit.ly/SIvS4S).

Easier.

Neater.

Quicker.

Safer-Less Dust

Stronger.

Cleaner.

BEST Litter Scoop Ever

I know it seems ridiculous that I would recommend a litter scoop, but seriously there is only one that I will ever use in my home and I have extras just in case! It's the Litter Lifter. It has peaked blades that allows the loose litter to fall back into the box. It is also huge and efficient, so it allows for less time and dust when cleaning the litter box(es).

You can see what I mean by watching this video about it (that features Charlie and Trigg!) (http://bit.ly/SlvSSt).

Stain and Odor Removal

Accidents happen. Especially when you're a little kitty! You can definitely get whatever you need off of your kitten with a wet paper towel or towel. Or just give them a bath with a pet safe shampoo.

However, what about your carpets and upholstery? If you live in an apartment or the like, then you may be even more concerned about cleaning up after your kitty. We have product tested Fizzion and have been very impressed by the results; you can see our review here (http://bit.ly/SlvYJL) and see the video of me product testing it here (http://bit.ly/Obju0M). I have also heard great things about Zero Odor.

Chapter 8

Dental Care – Teeth Brushing

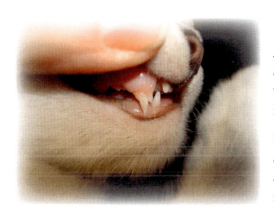

As with humans, it is important to start your kitten's dental regime early. Cat dentals can cost hundreds of dollars and sometimes thousands depending on what procedure needs to be done. It is best to start them early with teeth brushing.

I know it sounds ridiculous, but if you think about it, a cat in the wild that has just caught a mouse or a bird, has the benefit of the shearing off of heads and wings to clean their teeth.

This isn't so with a cat that is fed a commercial diet of dry or canned wet food – they are prone to gingivitis, holes in their teeth and even tartar. Contrary to popular belief, dry food is not necessarily better for cats' teeth.

The best time to start the teeth cleaning process is when they have their adult teeth in – at about 6-7 months of age (the photo above shows Trigg's baby canine and his adult canine growing in next to it – eventually his baby one was "pushed" out by his adult one). Of course, before that age, it won't hurt to start opening your cat's mouth and rubbing it's gums so that it will get used to you touching it's mouth and its teeth – be sure your hands are clean when you're doing it though!!

> The photo of Trigg's teeth in this chapter was taken when he was just 6 months old and you can see his adult canine growing in and his baby one in the process of falling out. I got Charlie and Trigg used to me touching their mouths at an early age.

Because a cat's tongue is pretty effective in cleaning the inside of the teeth, you will want to focus on the outside – along the gum line is where the worst patterns of disease seem to occur.

I recommend C.E.T. Toothpaste Poultry Flavor – it's a poultry flavored enzymatic toothpaste for use with cats as part of an essential program for the pet's oral health – you DO NOT want to use human toothpaste as it has fluoride and other things that a cat should not ingest – they do not have the ability to spit out food or their toothpaste, so it's safer to give them something they can consume.

Actually, Charlie and Trigg like all the flavors that C.E.T. Toothpaste comes in, so whether you pick Poultry, Beef or Salmon, your chances are pretty good that they'll love them!

Here is a video I took of brushing my parents' cat's Caymus' teeth (http://bit.ly/Olwv3z).

You can also read more about how to do brush your cat's teeth (http://bit.ly/Olwz37).

Of course, since you will see your vet shortly after your kitten comes home, it is a good idea to have your vet or a vet tech show you how to do this before starting it on your own.

You want to try and clean your cat's teeth twice a week; of course a daily routine would be even better. You want to brush about 30 second per side.

Conclusion

Maintaining a Healthy Ragdoll Cat

More than likely you will have many happy, healthy years ahead with your kitten. As I mentioned earlier, the average lifespan of a Ragdoll is 9-15 years, but many live way beyond 15 years of age.

Part of your cat's health and happiness will be to keep their home safe, peaceful, clean and healthy.

Be sure to scoop the litter box at least once a day.

Change their water once a day.

Clean the food bowl once a day.

Have a regular yearly vet check-up for your cat and keep vaccines up to date. KC Cat Clinic recommends two "Wellness" visits a year because 1 year in a cat's life can be like 9 in ours.

Trim front nails once every 3-4 weeks and back nails every 2 months or as needed.

Above all else, your kitty needs love and companionship and if you chose a Ragdoll – hopefully that's what you were going for as well because they are companions!

Thank You

A sincere thank you for reading *A Ragdoll Kitten Care Guide: Bringing Your Ragdoll Kitten Home*. It is my hope that you will share your kitty with us on Floppycats.com in the days, months and years to come. You are always welcomed to submit your kitty for Floppycats.com's Ragdoll of the Week (http://bit.ly/OlwyfC) once they are one-year old, as well. You might also consider submitting them for Ragdoll Kitten of the Month (http://bit.ly/ObjApj).

I would like to take this opportunity to say again that I spent a lot of time and effort creating this eBook and would appreciate it if you would respect my work by not sharing or distributing the eBook to anyone else without my permission.

If you would like to share this eBook with a friend, you can request they be sent an email. Just contact me through jenny@floppycats.com.

If you have any suggestions, tips or criticisms of this eBook, please do not hesitate to contact me at jenny@floppycats.com with any comments!

I am also always on the lookout for testimonials for the guide, if you are up for sending a testimonial, please think about the following questions and please let me know if you're game for a testimonial:

- What kind of doubts did you have before starting to read this guide? Be honest.
- How did the guide deliver on its promises?
- Who would you recommend this to and why?

You can stay up-to-date with all Ragdoll cat information, health concerns and product reviews by subscribing to our Floppycats Newsletter (http://bit.ly/SCDUk7), and to our daily blog posts and also by subscribing to our YouTube Channel (http://bit.ly/R4t7vG).

Bringing Your Ragdoll Kitten Home Checklist

o **Pet Carrier** – If your kitty is being shipped, then your kitten will come with one. If not, then you will want to get one to bring your kitten home in as well as use when going to the vet. Be sure carriers are large enough for when kittens get older- Medium size should be fine. Petmate Kennel Fashion Cab

o **Towel** - Have a towel or absorbent cloth for kitty to rest on, and in case of a potty accident, if he is in the carrier for a long time.

o **Food** – Get whatever your breeder recommends or is feeding them now.

o **Treats**   Whole Life Pet Treats, Honest Kitchen's Wishes as well as Eden Foods' Bonito Flakes

o **Water and Food Bowls** – I recommend stainless steel or ceramic ones for easy cleaning.

o **Litter Box** – Might as well get a big one like the PETCO Mega Rectangular Litter Box since your kitty will need it when s/he grows up. You might also bring one to the airport with you if your kitty is being flown to you. Caymus had a diarrhea attack all over my sister when we pulled him out of his carrier on the way home from the airport.

o **Litter**

o **Cat Toys** - Neko Flies, Yeowww! Catnip Banana, Bergan Turbo Scratcher, The Dog Spinny

o **Scratching Post** – Sisal – TopCat Products

o **Lounger/Bed/Scratcher** –

   o **Cardboard** – Bergan Turbo Scratcher, kittyblock, Petstages Snuggle Scratch and Rest, Brawny Cat or Imperial Cat Scratchers

   o **Sleepypod Crater Dot**

   o **PetStages Cuddle Coil** – great for quiet times, cat naps, play time and more!

o **Brush and Comb** - JW Pet Slicker Brush, JW Pet Comb, JW Pet Shedding Blade, Rakom Cat Grooming Tool

o **Nail Clippers** - JW Pet Company GripSoft Nail Clipper for Pets, Small

o **Additional recommendations from the breeder:**

Bonuses

How to Introduce Your New Ragdoll Kitten to a Resident Cat

Many people wonder how to introduce cats to each other. Cats are like people. Some will get along and some just might not ever get along. However, there are some things you can do, as a responsible pet owner, to make the transition with a new cat an easier one.

The first thing to remember is that your resident cat is going to feel like his or her area is being entrenched upon.

This is one of the reasons why you have set up a safe room for your new feline companion. Make sure that there are plenty of hiding places, a separate litter box, and separate food and water bowls in the safe room.

> You need to introduce your new cat into your household with care. The biggest mistake that most people make is forcing cats on one another right off the bat–like throwing them into the same room together and letting them "figure it out" on their own or simply opening your new cat's carrier and letting the new cat roam free without a proper introduction to your existing cat(s).

Block the door by either shutting it or putting baby gates up. If you decide to use the baby gates make sure that you put them on the inside of the door so you can also shut the door.

In fact, it is probably best to allow the new addition to spend at least 1-2 weeks in a room closed off from your other cats or cat. The reason for this is so that the new cat loses the smell of his or her previous home and gains the smell of your own. This is a crucial step.

Of course, your new cat will always have his or her distinct odor (that only kitties can smell), but as far as fur, etc. is concerned, it is best for the new one to have your home's smell on it as well as your smell on it. Also, you want to be sure that your new cat isn't bringing any diseases into the house and to your resident kitty. With a little patience, you can easily avoid a disaster.

Try not to stress your new addition. Bring them in a carrier and place the carrier in the safe room. Open the door and leave, giving them plenty of time to explore the safe room on their own. During this time your resident cat might sit outside the door and may occasionally hiss—smelling and hearing the new addition. Don't worry this is a normal reaction.

Once your resident cat has seemed to calm down a bit and does not seem so interested in the safe room door you can move to the next step. This could take a day or two, but patience is a virtue when it comes to the introduction process.

The next step is to introduce the cats to each others' scents. Take a clean pair of socks or wash cloths and rub each of the cats down with one. Make sure to rub their facial area where many of the scent glands are located. Next place the socks in the opposite cat's area, making sure not to put it close to their litter box or food and water bowls.

Sprinkle both cats with baby powder and brush it out. This will help everyone smell the same. Then, take a soft cloth and wipe it around the new cat/kitten's face, under the chin, ear to ear, where some of the scent glands are located. Next, one at a time, alternating between new kitten and any of the existing cats, wipe around their faces in the same area. This exchanges scents and makes them more aware of the other cat's smell without actually having to get close to do so. This is also good to use when one comes home from spending time at the vet or a cat show.

You can also achieve this by switching the cats' areas. For example, let your resident cat have time smelling the safe room and your new cat spend time smelling and exploring the house. It is probably a good idea to remove the litter boxes and food and water bowls so there is no hard feelings when the rooms are switched back. Cats are very sensitive to other cats' urine smells. Be sure to introduce all smells.

Patience is key during the introduction stage since one bad reaction could cause long term damage in the cats' relationship.

Depending on how your cats react to this it might be time to move to the next step. Using a baby gate barrier it is time to open the door and let the cats see each other. They will most definitely be curious about each other. Watch their reactions to each other. If there is any hissing or growling then it is important to take this step slowly.

When the isolation period is over, bring both cats (one person brings the new cat and one person brings the resident kitty) to the largest room of the house. The new cat is on one end of the room, whereas the older cat is on the other end of the room. Whether you are handling the new cat or resident cat, be sure to do non-threatening things, like playing or petting them, allowing both cats to eye each other. You want to desensitize them to the other's presence. You can also feed them something yummy, or comb or brush them if that's what they like. You want both cats to see each other without making aggressive behavior or have aggressive posturing.

Once the cats seem to be calm at the sight of each other it is probably safe to introduce the two. Make sure that they are supervised during this initial meeting. If there is any problems during this time go back a step, allowing them to view each other on opposite sides of the baby gate.

When they encounter each other where they stay calm and not angry, it encourages them to interact this way again the next time they meet. If they do well for a short time at a great distance, the next day repeat the process by decreasing the distance between them by a foot or two and increase the time they have to check each other out. On the first day start about 10 feet apart for five minutes, the next day try eight feet apart for 10 minutes and so on and so forth. This is a proper approach of how to introduce new cats to your household. If they start being aggressive, you will have to back up and start over. I know it sounds tedious, but believe me, it's worth it!

If several days go by and you feel like they are tolerating each other, let them explore the room and find each other at their own speed. There will be some degree of posturing between them in order to figure out who's who. Ideally you would like for them to be able to be in the same room or on the same piece of furniture without fighting. Realistic expectations are for them to tolerate one another. If you're lucky, then they may turn out to really like or love one another.

If things go well you can allow them to spend longer and longer amounts of time together until they are together full time. For the first couple of weeks you might want to provide two food and water bowls and separate litter boxes just in case one decides to get territorial.

There is no sure-fire way to tell if cats will be friends for life. Like people, there will be some that just don't mesh. Slow introductions are an important step in doing what you can to ease the tension of the new addition.

Cats don't like to meet other cats and immediately begin playing, like most dogs. On the contrary, they like to approach each other cautiously, establishing their social position with confrontation, a key part of how to introduce new cats to your household. Inter-cat aggression may result in fighting, stalking, inappropriate litter box behavior, and in general, just making one of the cat's lives miserable.

Some cats, no matter how hard you try, are not going to accept new cats into a household. Sometimes your vet can recommend medication to make them less anxious and relieve some of the problems. Your vet can also advise other behavior modification techniques to take the stress off. If you feel like there are problems, talk to your vet immediately about solutions of how to introduce new cats to your household. The longer you wait, the worse it could get.

Many Floppycats' readers have reported that Feliway Plug-In Diffusers work well. The ingredients in Feliway simulate your cat's natural pheromones to help your pet cope with stress. You can just plug it into any wall socket.

How We Introduced 15-year old Rags to Two Ragdoll Kittens

When we introduced Caymus and Murphy to Rags, we were very careful in our approach. Rags was 15-years old at the time, and we had already tried to introduce him to a cat, Kit-Kat, we rescued from the Humane Society about eight years before. At that time, Rags took a dump in the middle of everyone's bed (except for mine) and starting peeing all over the place. We eventually had to find another home for Kit-Kat. So, we knew that introducing him to two kittens eight years later would be a challenge. However, the vet did mention that he would probably be more tolerant of them because he was older (and probably more accepting), but that getting two kittens would be better than one. Two kittens could play with each other without bothering Rags all that much. These are all things to consider when properly introducing new cats to your household. We put Caymus and Murphy in a separate room - where Rags only had access to them under a door.

They spent two weeks in that room—acquiring the smells of our home and of us— before Rags was introduced to them. It was one of the hardest things to do as we were eager for them to meet and we wondered what they would do. Yet, it was an essential part of how to properly introduce new cats to our household. We had to make sure they would be okay because my father had already warned us that he thought it would be a bad idea to bring in two more cats.

When the two weeks were up, we put the kittens in a carrier and let Rags in the room. He had the power and control because they were locked up. He was the one that was able to approach them. Once he smelled them and did his hissing, and finally settled on a bed across the room where he could keep an eye on them, we let them out. He watched them interact, as they were a little too young to notice him in the room. We repeated this process over and over again. We kept the kittens in that room for probably 2-3 months before letting them out for good, always giving Rags the proper amount of attention and affection, so that he was not jealous of their homecoming. I am happy to report - there was neither inter-cat aggression nor peeing/pooping in the wrong spots!

Questions to Ask Ragdoll Breeders

If you are thinking of adopting a Ragdoll kitten, here are the right questions for cat breeders to ensure you are choosing the right breeder.

Something to keep in mind is that a responsible Ragdoll breeder should ALSO be interviewing the buyer (customer/you) to be sure that the breeder is selling to a qualified, loving family (if the breeder just wants a deposit without talking/interviewing a buyer to be qualified to home one of their babies, then there should be red flags- they may just want your money)! If they do not interview and qualify a buyer, what would that say about how they are raising the kittens? They need to care about where their fur baby is going as well.

1. How long have you been breeding Ragdolls?
Ideally, you're looking for someone who has been breeding Ragdolls long enough to know what they are doing. Also, I look for breeders that concentrate on Ragdolls. I am crazy about Ragdolls, and I want my breeder to be also!

2. How did you pick Ragdolls to breed?
Again, you are looking for someone who is interested in the Ragdoll breed for a good reason.

3. Do you show? Why or why not?
This is a touchy one for me. I really don't care if the cats are shown, but I do care if they are interested in spending time with their cats and playing with them.

4. What congenital defects are in Ragdolls?
Breeders should be knowledgeable enough to know what defects the Ragdoll breed carries and how to minimize them in their breeding. They should be up front with you. As any pure bred will have its problems.

5. How are you breeding to avoid those defects?
See Above

6. How large is your breeding operation?
I prefer smaller breeding operations because then the breeder has more time to

spend with their litters and get them more people-orientated. Usually, the less the number of cats, the healthier the living conditions will be.

7. Where do your cats spend most of their time?
You're wondering if the cats get socialized properly. After all, one of the benefits in getting a cat from a breeder is knowing its history and knowing if it's been exposed to dogs, other cats, birds, etc.

8. Do you breed full time? In other words, do you have another job?
I prefer breeders that breed full time, as you know they are concentrating on what they are doing. However, there are excellent breeders that have full time jobs as well. So this answer alone isn't a reason to eliminate a breeder.

9. What sort of health guarantees do you offer?
Your breeder should offer some sort of health guarantee, but no breeder (even the very best) can offer a 100% health guarantee. Some breeders will replace the kitten, should it develop a disease or defect as listed on their health guarantee.

Kittens should come with a sales contract with guarantees, and not "word of mouth" guarantees or health guarantees, etc. All should be in writing.

10. What happens if the kitten gets sick?
This should be listed on the health guarantee. Also, the kitten should have seen a vet before coming to you.

11. Do you have any fun adoption stories to share?
This will show you how much the breeder enjoys the adoption process and feels passionate about what they do.

12. What makes this kitten or cat "pet quality" or "show quality"?
This isn't terribly important, unless it is important to you. "Show Quality" just means that the cat has the proper markings as designated by the CFA or TICA.

13. Do you keep some of your cats for your own?
This shows you whether or not the breeder is doing the breeding for a business or as a business and a hobby. You want the ones that do it as a hobby too, as that means they truly enjoy it.

14. How old is your oldest cat that you've bred?
This gives me an idea of the longevity of the breeder's lines.

15. What is your favorite Ragdoll look?
I usually ask this one out of curiosity. The breeder that likes seals like me is going to predominately breed seals.

16. May I speak with three people who own your cats?
The breeder should have this list ready to go because you always want to ask for referrals!

17. Do you raise your cats underfoot?
This means, "Are the cats raised in your home with you, free to roam?"

Some poor breeding cats are unfortunately raised in cages but the cats are still "technically" in the breeder's home. So sometimes the kittens might be raised underfoot, but the breeding cats are not.

You could additionally ask if a breeder cages any of their cats and if so, why? How big are the cages, if any? (a large 10 by 5 by 6 foot "run" for a breeder boy only, so he can be around other cats instead of in his own room, etc. and the "girls" run free in the house)?

If they have a separate building so cats are not all in the home, there should be the ability for, at least, the girls to run free, perhaps another room for them if they go into heat (when they may spray) and a separate but comfy large area or room for the male(s) to live-where they are not caged. Boys HAVE to be separated from the girls or else there is no control of who and when the girls get pregnant.

Some breeders have a separate part of the house or separate building in their backyard where they keep the cats. If the cats are raised underfoot, most likely, they will be used to sounds like the dishwasher, the washing machine, the vacuum, etc. before they come to you. I would recommend underfoot cats only.

Responsible breeders keep their cats as loved pets first, and breeders second.

18. Can you send photos of the parents before I adopt a kitten? Or do you post the parents on the website?

The breeder should be more than happy to show off the two cats that she or he decided to breed to make your fabulous kitten. You should see if you like the look of the kitten's parents to be sure-the kitten will have the look you desire.

Many breeders do not post either their breeding cats' pictures online or the parents' pedigree. (A lot of breeders don't include all their breeding cats online, or their cats' full names – so then you don't know where the cats are from/what lines.)

In my opinion a Ragdoll breeder should have all of their breeding cats and their pedigrees online. This is important to see that the kittens have not been inbred and the pedigree shows at least three generations (of Ragdolls) listed so you know the parents are true Ragdolls.

19. Do you send the kitten's pedigree when you adopt a kitten?

You are, after all, purchasing a pure bred kitten. You should care about their pedigree.

20. Will it be a problem if I request, and want to pay for, the DNA testing before I accept a kitten?

You might want to do this to make sure your kitten is healthy. If you are planning on breeding your kitten–and buying breeding rights to it, then you absolutely need to have this done to make sure the Ragdoll lines stay healthy.

Ragdolls can be gene tested for color (carrying chocolate) and some other tests at VGL http://www.vgl.ucdavis.edu/services/cat/ and for the best cardiac genetics would be Washington State University, WSU (Dr. Meurs who is doing Ragdoll Gene testing) http://www.vetmed.wsu.edu/deptsvcgl/ResearchFeline.aspx. I understand Dr. Meurs "may" be relocating her lab in the future but this is the site for qualified cardiac testing.

21. Can I visit your cattery?

If a cattery is clean and organized, then a breeder should allow you to visit and see where you kitty comes from. If they are opposed to it, red flags should go up–and you might wonder what they are trying to hide. However, there is a distinction between a "kitten visit" and a "cattery visit". Some breeders might have their cattery incorporated into their home and may not be comfortable allowing perfect strangers to go through their home. However, they may be okay with you staying in their living room, for example, to meet a kitten you've seen on their website that you're interested in. It is important to understand that some breeders are protective of their homes. So be sure to get clarity. Even by visiting their living room, you can learn a lot about their cleanliness and their cats (if their house cats are interested in you and hanging around or if they are scared and hiding).

22. If a possible adoptee cannot visit your cattery, are you willing to talk to your adoptee on the phone?
If the breeder is unwilling to take the time for a phone conversation, what will she/he be like when you have a problem?

23. How do you honor your health guarantee?
The breeder should be willing to pay for the vet bills associated with the claims made in the guarantee or take the kitten back and offer you a replacement.

24. What if a kitten gets adopted and the customer is unhappy with a kitten, what do you do?
The breeder should take the kitten back–if she or he cares about her or his cats and their well-being

25. How are your kittens registered?
For example, if you want to show in CFA, in order for a kitten to be CFA registered, the parents and cattery have to be CFA registered. If they're not, you have to go through a process of registering via pedigree, which is a little more time consuming.

The kittens should have their *litter registered* with CFA or TICA so the parents should also be registered with one or the other. Buyers should get the kitten's "registry papers" to fill out from either CFA and/or TICA (OR other reputable cat associations, if not in the USA such as FIFE.) If you do not get registration papers from the breeder for your kitten, how can you know that it is a real pedigreed, registered Ragdoll that you are buying?

26. Are you capable of including the kitten's maturing pattern since birth?
This is a good measure about how much attention and time is spent with the kittens.

27. What vaccination brand do you use? And what vaccinations are given, when?
This will help you know the research the breeder does and the quality of their vet–be sure to double check with your own vet and see what s/he thinks of that brand.

28. What are the kittens fed?

Again, this is a good measure of how important the cat's health is to the breeder. If the breeder is feeding grocery store bought food, like Meow Mix, more than likely, their cats' health isn't the first priority and should draw red flags for you.

…and ABOVE ALL, you should be able to ask for as many photos and ask as many questions as you need to, so that you feel comfortable with the huge decision you are about to make. After all, if your new kitten lives as long as Rags, then you are making over a 19-year commitment to an animal! There should be no doubt in your mind that this is the right breeder and right kitten.

39484922R00036

Made in the USA
Middletown, DE
16 January 2017

Made in the USA
San Bernardino, CA
12 February 2018